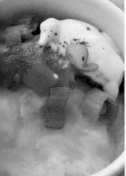

## Mealtime is just a mug away!

# MUG SHOTS

Printed in the United States of America
by G&R Publishing Co.

Distributed By:

**CQ Products**

507 Industrial Street
Waverly, IA 50677

ISBN-13: 978-1-56383-527-8
Item #3020

# IT MAY BE TIME FOR A MUG SHOT

**IF...**

*You currently own a mug*
*Your microwave is in working condition*
*You have a few minutes to spare*
*You want a quick single-serving meal*
*You love delicious food*

## Quick Tips

**1** Make sure your mug is safe to use in the microwave. How? Turn the mug over. It should say "microwave safe." If it doesn't, fill the mug with water and microwave on the highest setting for 1 minute. If the mug is cool enough to handle, it's safe to use; if not, try another mug. Never microwave a mug with metallic decorations.

**2** For safety sake, always use hot pads when removing anything from the microwave. Even if your mug isn't hot, the contents are, and you just don't want to take the chance of burning yourself.

**3** Follow quantities and cooking times for each recipe. Times may vary slightly depending on your microwave and your mug. All recipes in this book were tested in a 1,000-watt microwave, and the mug size used for testing is listed in each recipe.

**4** Enjoy your delicious mug meals hot from the microwave, right from the mug.

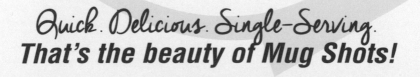

*Quick. Delicious. Single-Serving.*
***That's the beauty of Mug Shots!***

# Kielbasa & Rice

½ C. quick-cooking
white rice

1 to 2 T. dry bearnaise
sauce mix *(or other
white sauce mix)*

6 grape tomatoes, halved

½ tsp. dried minced onion

½ tsp. chopped
fresh chives

3 T. milk

½ C. chicken broth

⅓ C. diced kielbasa

Black pepper to taste

## Directions

Place the uncooked rice in a greased mug. Add dry sauce mix, tomato halves, minced onion, chopped chives, milk, chicken broth, and diced kielbasa; give it a quick stir.

Microwave on high until it starts bubbling around the edges, then cook 90 seconds longer.

Cover with foil and let stand 5 minutes until the rice is nice and tender. Sprinkle with a little black pepper and give it a stir before eating. MUG

*Kielbasa is a type of Polish sausage. It's readily available, but you can use any type of Polish or smoked sausage instead.* TIP

Mug Tested
14 oz.

5

# Fruity PB Oatmeal

½ small ripe banana, mashed

½ small apple, chopped

⅓ C. quick-cooking oats

¾ to 1 C. milk

½ tsp. ground cinnamon

2 tsp. creamy peanut butter

1 tsp. brown sugar

## Directions

Put the mashed banana and chopped apple into a greased mug. Add uncooked oats and ¾ cup milk. Stir in the cinnamon, peanut butter, and brown sugar until well combined.

Microwave on high for 2 minutes; stir. Microwave 1 minute more. Stir in the remaining ¼ cup milk if you want thinner oatmeal. Add toppings, if you'd like. MUG

*Yogurt, honey, granola, chopped nuts, coconut, and/or extra fruit all make great toppings.*

# Chili & Cornbread

Pour ½ C. prepared chili into a greased mug. In a small bowl, combine ¾ tsp. sugar, 2 T. flour, 2 T. cornmeal, a pinch of salt, and ½ tsp. baking powder. In a separate bowl, beat 1 egg white until foamy. Add 2 T. milk, 1 tsp. vegetable oil, and 1 T. taco sauce to the egg white; stir until well blended. Fold in 2 tsp. cream-style corn, 1 tsp. canned chopped green chiles, and 1 T. shredded Mexican cheese blend. Combine wet and dry ingredients, stirring until just blended; slowly pour the mixture over the chili in the mug. Cover with a paper towel and microwave on high for 2½ minutes or until the cornbread tests done with a toothpick. Yum-yum! MUG

# Banana Bread

In a greased mug, stir together 3½ T. flour, 2 tsp. sugar, and 2 T. brown sugar. In a small bowl, stir together ⅛ tsp. each salt, baking powder, and baking soda and add to flour mixture; stir to combine. Add ¼ C. egg substitute, ¼ tsp. vanilla, 1 T. vegetable oil, and 1 T. half & half, stirring until well blended. Fold in ½ mashed ripe banana and 1 T. raisins; scrape down the side of the mug. Microwave on high for 2 to 2½ minutes or until a sharp knife inserted through the bread to the bottom of the mug comes out nearly clean. Spread Nutella, peanut butter, or cream cheese over the top, if you'd like. **MUG**

# All-in-One Breakfast

½ C. frozen shredded
hash browns

⅓ C. egg substitute

2 T. shredded sharp
cheddar cheese, divided

1 frozen heat-and-serve
sausage patty, thawed &
cut into pieces

1 T. water

Salt & black pepper to taste

## Directions

Toss frozen hash browns into a greased mug.

Microwave on high for 60 seconds. Pour in the egg
substitute. Add 1 tablespoon cheese, the sausage pieces,
water, salt, and black pepper; stir it all together.

Microwave on high for 45 seconds and stir again. Sprinkle
on the remaining 1 tablespoon cheese and microwave
60 seconds more or until set. MUG

It may be just one serving, but you can
still make it special. Go ahead and garnish
with extra cheese and fresh herbs. TIP

# Veggie-Stuffed Pepper

1 red bell pepper

½ C. stewed tomatoes
   with juice

2½ T. quick-cooking
   brown rice

1 T. hot water

1 green onion, thinly sliced

¼ C. frozen corn kernels,
   thawed

¼ C. black beans,
   drained & rinsed

¼ tsp. red pepper flakes

Salt & black pepper to taste

¼ C. shredded
   mozzarella cheese

1½ tsp. grated
   Parmesan cheese

## Directions

Cut around the stem of the bell pepper; toss out the stem, seeds, and ribs. Pop the pepper into an ungreased mug, cover with vented plastic wrap, and microwave on high for 2 minutes or until tender.

In another mug, mix tomatoes, uncooked rice, and water. Cover with vented plastic wrap and set on a double layer of paper towels in the microwave. Microwave on high for 3½ minutes or until rice is tender. Stir in the sliced green onion, thawed corn, rinsed beans, pepper flakes, salt, and black pepper.

Pack the tomato mixture into the bell pepper, cover with vented plastic wrap, and microwave on high for 1 to 2 minutes or until heated through. (Remember, even vented plastic wrap traps steam, so remove it carefully!)

Sprinkle both cheeses over the top of the pepper and let it stand there a few minutes so the cheese has a chance to melt a bit. MUG

# Angel Alfredo

⅓ C. broken angel hair pasta*

½ C. lukewarm water

1 tsp. butter

2½ T. dry Alfredo sauce mix

1 tsp. dried parsley

¼ tsp. rosemary garlic seasoning

¼ C. plus 2 T. milk

## Directions

Put uncooked pasta pieces and water in an ungreased mug and set it on a double layer of paper towels in the microwave.

Microwave on high until it boils and then boil for 60 seconds. Be prepared – it will boil over. Just let it do its thing. Stir in the butter, dry sauce mix, parsley, seasoning, and milk; stir lightly.

Microwave on high for 90 seconds. Stir it up again and let it set there for a minute so it thickens up a bit, then dig in! MUG

* Break the pasta so the pieces lie relatively flat in your mug.

Mug Tested
8 oz.

# Pumpkin & Chip Muffin

3 T. flour

1 T. pumpkin puree

Pinch or two of
   pumpkin pie spice

Pinch of salt

¼ tsp. baking powder

1 T. dark chocolate chips

1 T. sugar

1 T. milk

1 tsp. canola oil

¼ tsp. vanilla

Cinnamon-sugar

## Directions

In a greased mug, stir together the flour, pumpkin puree, pumpkin pie spice, salt, baking powder, chocolate chips, sugar, milk, oil, and vanilla; scrape down the side of the mug. Smooth the top of the batter a wee bit and give it a hefty sprinkle of cinnamon-sugar.

Microwave on high for 60 seconds. Check it with a toothpick; it should be done, but if not, just give it another ride on the microwave carousel and watch it go around and around for 15 seconds or so.

## Keep some on hand

Stir together 2½ C. flour, ¾ tsp. pumpkin pie spice, ¾ tsp. salt, 1 T. baking powder, ¼ C. dark chocolate chips, and ¾ C. sugar; store in an airtight container. Make mounds of pumpkin puree *(1 T. each)* and place on a waxed paper-lined tray; cover and freeze. To make 1 muffin, stir together about ⅓ C. muffin mix, 1 T. milk, 1 tsp. oil, ¼ tsp. vanilla, and 1 pie filling mound *(thawed)* in a greased mug. Sprinkle with cinnamon-sugar and microwave as directed above. MUG

# Personal Pizza

2 T. self-rising flour

⅛ tsp. Italian seasoning

1½ T. milk

½ tsp. olive oil

Pizza sauce or salsa

Cooked & crumbled Italian sausage

Sliced black olives

Shredded mozzarella cheese

## Directions

Grease a mug. Toss in the flour and Italian seasoning. Stir in the milk and oil. Scrape down the side of the mug and spread the dough evenly in the bottom; let stand for 2 minutes.

Pour a little pizza sauce over the dough. Layer the cooked sausage, olives, and cheese on top.

Microwave on high for 2 minutes or until the dough is thoroughly cooked. MUG

It may be small, but this pizza packs in lots of flavor. Customize your pizza with toppings of your choice for a versatile mini meal. TIP

# Raspberry Pancake

Fresh raspberries

5 T. self-rising flour

1¾ tsp. sugar

⅓ C. plus 1 T. milk

1¾ tsp. melted butter

## Directions

Grease a mug and put in enough raspberries to cover the bottom.

In a small bowl, stir together the flour, sugar, milk, and butter. Pour this mixture slowly over the berries in the mug.

Microwave on high for 90 seconds. Test for doneness with a toothpick. If it comes out with a few dry crumbs, it's done. If it needs more time, microwave in 15-second intervals until it tests done. **MUG**

*TIP*

*You can make this recipe with any type of berry or fruit. Then top it off with anything you like on a pancake.*

# Party Ranch Potatoes

Put 1 C. frozen shredded hash browns in an ungreased mug. Add 1 T. cream cheese *(cut up)*, 1½ tsp. sour cream, 1 tsp. dried chopped chives, 1 tsp. dry ranch dip seasoning, 1 T. bacon bits, ¼ C. milk, and ½ T. butter. Cover with vented plastic wrap and microwave on high for 4 minutes. Uncover carefully. Stir well. Eat. Enjoy. **MUG**

Mug Tested
*8 oz.*

# Quick Baked Beans

Put 1 (8 oz.) can pork and beans in a greased mug. Stir in
1 T. brown sugar, 4 Little Smokies *(chopped)*, 2 tsp. lemonade
powder *(not sugar-free)*, 1 tsp. dried minced onion, and
½ tsp. dry mustard. Microwave on high for 90 seconds; stir.
Microwave 90 seconds more; stir again and toss on a few
green onion slices, if you'd like. *(The lemonade powder is a
delicious addition, and even cheese-filled Little Smokies taste
good in these beans!)* **MUG**

# Mug Shot Meatloaf

2 T. milk

1 T. ketchup, plus
   more for serving

2 T. quick-cooking oats

1 heaping tsp. dry onion
   soup mix

¼ lb. lean ground beef

## Directions

In a small bowl, combine milk, 1 tablespoon ketchup, uncooked oats, and soup mix. Crumble beef into the bowl and mix well. Press the mixture gently into an ungreased mug.

Microwave on high for 2½ to 3 minutes or until meat is no longer pink. Top with additional ketchup, if you'd like. MUG

You might want to try making this recipe with BBQ sauce, chili sauce, or even pizza sauce in place of the ketchup. TIP

# Fiesta Mac & Cheese

½ C. big elbow macaroni

½ C. plus 1 T. warm water

Pinch of salt

1 tsp. flour

3 T. milk *(room temperature)*

¼ C. plus 1 T. shredded sharp cheddar cheese

1 tsp. butter

2 T. fire-roasted tomato salsa

## Directions

In a greased mug, combine the uncooked macaroni, ½ cup water, and salt. Set your mug on a double layer of paper towels in the microwave.

Microwave on high for 2 minutes. Now give it a quick stir. Microwave 2 minutes longer, and then stir again. It's going to boil over; don't worry. Add the remaining 1 tablespoon water before microwaving 60 seconds more or until the macaroni is al dente; stir.

Sprinkle the flour over the cooked macaroni. Add the milk, cheese, butter, and salsa, but don't stir. Microwave on high for 30 seconds and then give it a gentle stir. Microwave 30 seconds more, if needed, until the cheese is melted and everything is nice and creamy. MUG

*Change it up by adding 2 T. crumbled dried shiitake mushrooms along with the macaroni and replacing the salsa with your favorite pesto.*

# Curry Chicken

1 T. thinly sliced green onion

½ tsp. curry powder

⅓ C. water

2½ T. quick-cooking couscous

2½ T. frozen peas, partially thawed

¼ C. cubed cooked chicken

2 T. mayonnaise

2 T. chopped red bell pepper

1 to 2 T. sweet mango chutney

Pita chips

## Directions

Put sliced green onion, curry powder, water, and uncooked couscous in a greased mug. Microwave on high until it boils.

Stir in partially thawed peas, cubed chicken, mayonnaise, chopped bell pepper, and chutney. Cover with vented plastic wrap and cook at 70% power for 3 minutes or until couscous is tender.

Serve with pita chips. MUG

*Trapped steam burns! Remove the plastic wrap carefully.*

# Anytime Cup-a-Quiche

2 eggs

3 T. milk

Salt & black pepper to taste

½ plain bagel

1 T. plus 1 tsp. cream cheese

¼ C. chopped cooked ham

Fresh chives, chopped

## Directions

Break eggs into a greased mug and pour in milk; add salt and black pepper and whisk until well blended.

Cut bagel and cream cheese into ½" pieces and add to the egg mixture. Stir in the chopped ham. Sprinkle chives on top.

Microwave on high for 2½ to 3 minutes or until eggs are set. MUG

*Try using flavored cream cheese instead of plain or add a little shredded cheese, cooked bacon, or other herbs, if you'd like.*

# Veggie 'Roni Lasagna

1 oven-ready lasagna noodle

Warm water

3 T. pasta sauce

¼ C. cottage cheese

1 T. sun-dried tomato pesto

¼ C. chopped kale

2 stuffed green olives, sliced

4 pepperoni slices

½ C. shredded mozzarella cheese

## Directions

Pour water into a wide shallow bowl. Break the lasagna noodle in half crosswise and submerge both halves in the water. Let soak about 5 minutes or until flexible.

Pour half the pasta sauce in the bottom of a greased mug. Shake excess water from one noodle piece and lay it over the sauce, folding the edges of the noodle down over itself. Spread half the cottage cheese over the noodle, followed by half the pesto. Place half the kale over the pesto, and then layer on half each of the olive slices, pepperoni slices, and cheese. Repeat layers. Drizzle 1 teaspoon of the soaking water over the top. Cover with vented plastic wrap.

Microwave at 70% power for 2 minutes or until noodle pieces are tender. MUG

*You can put a bunch of these together assembly line-style and keep them covered in your refrigerator for several days until you have a hankerin' for more.*

TIP

# Chicken & Stuffing

2 T. cream of celery soup

2 T. cream of potato soup

2 T. canned peas & carrots, drained

1 (5 oz.) can chunk chicken breast, drained

Salt & black pepper to taste

½ C. dry Stove Top stuffing mix *(any flavor)*

¼ C. water

1 T. butter

Dried parsley to taste

## Directions

In a greased mug, stir together both soups, drained veggies, drained chicken, salt, and black pepper.

In a small bowl, stir together dry stuffing mix, water, butter, and parsley; put on top of the chicken mixture and cover with vented plastic wrap.

Microwave on high for 3 minutes or until stuffing is tender and everything is nice and hot. MUG

 TIP

*Put together several of these, cover, and freeze without microwaving. Just thaw and then heat as directed above.*

# French Onion Soup

In an ungreased mug, combine ½ C. thinly sliced onion and ¼ C. butter. Microwave on high for 90 seconds. Add ¼ C. sliced mushrooms and microwave 90 seconds more. Pour in ¾ C. beef broth, 1 T. dry white wine, and ¼ tsp. Worcestershire sauce. Add black pepper to taste. Microwave on high for 1 to 2 minutes or until onion is tender, then stir. Set a small piece of toasted French bread on the soup and top with a little shredded Swiss cheese and Parmesan cheese. Microwave on high for 20 seconds or until cheese is melted. Good things come from a mug! **MUG**

# Potato Soup

Toss 1 C. unpeeled cubed red potato *(about 1 medium)* into an ungreased mug; microwave on high for 2 minutes, stirring halfway through cooking time. Stir in ⅓ C. chicken broth and ¼ C. milk. Microwave at 50% power for 4 to 5 minutes or until tender, stirring every minute or two. Mash potatoes lightly with a fork *(you still want some small pieces in there)*. Stir in 1 bacon strip *(cooked & crumbled)* and 2 T. shredded cheddar cheese. Add sliced green onion, garlic salt, and black pepper to taste; stir to combine. Hot and satisfying anytime. MUG

# Monkey in a Mug

1 T. butter

½ tsp. cinnamon

2 T. sugar

1 (6-ct.) tube refrigerated buttermilk biscuits

## Directions

Melt butter in a small bowl. In another small bowl, stir together cinnamon and sugar.

Remove 2 or 3 biscuits from the tube. *(Immediately wrap the tube – with the remaining biscuits still inside it – tightly in plastic wrap and foil; refrigerate until you're ready to make more.)* Cut each biscuit into four even pieces and dip in butter, then in the cinnamon-sugar mixture. Set coated pieces in a greased mug.

Microwave on high for 60 seconds. That's it! Eat it while it's hot, and stir it up while you're eating because you'll find lots of cinnamon-y goodness at the bottom of the mug.

## Salted Caramel Monkey in a Mug

Dip biscuit pieces in melted butter and then in a combination of ½ tsp. cinnamon, 1 T. sugar, 1 T. brown sugar, and ¼ tsp. coarse salt. As you place biscuit pieces in your mug, sprinkle on just a tiny bit more coarse salt. Microwave as directed above. Before eating, drizzle with your favorite caramel sauce. Over-the-top good! MUG

# Mexicali Eggs

2 eggs

2 T. shredded Mexican
cheese blend, divided

1 T. bacon bits

⅛ tsp. chili powder,
or more to taste

1 T. salsa, any variety,
plus more for serving

Sour cream

Sliced green onion

## Directions

Break eggs into a greased mug and whisk well. Add
1 tablespoon cheese, the bacon bits, chili powder, and
1 tablespoon salsa; whisk until everything is well blended.

Microwave on high for 60 seconds, stir it up, and then
microwave 30 seconds more until eggs are set. Top with
remaining 1 tablespoon cheese.

Drizzle more salsa over the top, add a dollop of sour cream,
and toss on some green onion slices. MUG

 You can also remove the cooked
Mexicali Eggs from the mug and roll
them up in a flour tortilla.

# Shrimp & Fennel Noodles

½ (3 oz.) pkg. shrimp flavor ramen noodles

3 T. hot water

½ fennel bulb, trimmed & thinly sliced

½ tsp. minced garlic

Salt & black pepper to taste

1 T. butter

8 large frozen cooked shrimp, thawed

1 tsp. sherry cooking wine

Paprika to taste

## Directions

Break up the noodles and place them in an ungreased mug; drizzle with water and stir lightly. Add the fennel slices and garlic. Sprinkle with half the ramen seasoning packet and as much salt and black pepper as you'd like. Top with butter.

Cover with plastic wrap and microwave at 50% power for 2 minutes; stir. Microwave at 50% power 2 minutes longer or until fennel is soft. Add shrimp to the mug and stir gently. Drizzle with sherry and sprinkle with paprika.

Cover and microwave on high for 60 seconds or until shrimp are hot and noodles are tender. MUG

You'll find fennel in the produce aisle. The bulb, stalk, leaves, and seeds are all edible. Surprisingly, their taste is different than their aroma.

TIP

# Tropical Salmon & Rice

½ C. quick-cooking white rice

1 tsp. chicken bouillon granules

1 tsp. dried parsley

1 T. chopped dried mango

1 T. chopped pecans

⅓ C. hot water

2 to 3 T. orange juice *(or an orange & tropical fruit juice blend)*

1 T. olive oil

1 (5 oz.) can salmon, drained

## Directions

In a greased mug, mix uncooked rice, bouillon granules, parsley, and chopped mango and pecans. Stir in water, juice, and oil.

Microwave on high for 2 minutes; stir. Cover with foil and let stand for 3 minutes or until rice is tender. Stir in salmon. MUG

*You can replace the dried mango with dried pineapple, or use raisins instead and replace the salmon with canned chunk chicken breast.*

# Tots 'n' Ham Au Gratin

1 tsp. butter

1 T. chopped onion

1½ tsp. flour

Salt & black pepper to taste

2 T. half & half

2 T. milk

1 C. frozen mini tater tots

¼ C. diced ham

¼ C. diced celery

2 slices American cheese, diced

## Directions

Put the butter and chopped onion in a greased mug. Cover with a paper towel and microwave on high for 1 minute.

Sprinkle flour, salt, and black pepper over the top of the onion and then whisk in the half & half and milk.

Microwave uncovered on high for 30 seconds; let stand 2 minutes and then stir. Toss in the frozen tater tots and diced ham and celery. Cover with vented plastic wrap and microwave on high for 3 minutes.

Carefully uncover and stir in the diced cheese. Cover again with vented plastic wrap and microwave on high for 60 seconds or until everything is hot and the cheese is melted. MUG

*Covering the mug with a paper towel simply prevents the butter from splattering in your nice clean microwave.*

TIP

# Popeye Pasta

⅓ C. frozen chopped spinach, thawed

½ C. rotini pasta

Pinch of salt

⅔ C. plus 1 T. water

½ C. canned diced Italian tomatoes with juice

⅓ C. canned chickpeas, drained & rinsed

2 T. diced cooked turkey or ham

2 T. feta cheese crumbles

Black pepper to taste

## Directions

Drain spinach and press to remove any excess moisture; fluff with a fork and set aside.

In a greased mug, combine uncooked pasta, salt, and water; set the mug on several layers of paper towels in the microwave. Microwave on high for 2 minutes and then stir. Microwave on high 3 minutes more. You're gonna lose most *(or all)* of your water. That's ok. Just add the remaining 1 tablespoon water and microwave 2 minutes longer or until pasta is tender.

Stir in the tomatoes, drained chickpeas, diced turkey, and drained spinach. Pop it in the microwave once more for 60 to 90 seconds or until heated through. Let stand for 60 seconds before stirring in the cheese. Sprinkle with black pepper. MUG

*Popeye was definitely on to something! Spinach is loaded with nutrients and flavonoids and is heart-healthy and delicious, too.*

Mug Tested
12 oz.

# Cinnamon Roll Single

Remove 1 roll and the frosting packet from a tube of refrigerated Grands cinnamon rolls. *(Immediately wrap the tube – with the remaining rolls still inside it – tightly in plastic wrap and foil; refrigerate until you're ready to make another roll.)* Set the single roll in a greased mug and microwave on high for 60 seconds or until no longer doughy. Drizzle with a little of the frosting. One of the simplest sweet breakfast treats you can make in a mug! **MUG**

50

# Grab 'n' Go French Toast

Cut two bread slices *(we used cinnamon-raisin)* into 1" cubes and dump them into a greased mug; press down gently. In a small bowl, beat 2 T. egg substitute with 3 T. half & half and ½ tsp. cinnamon-sugar; pour it over the bread and press down gently again. Let stand a minute or two. Microwave for 75 seconds or until the egg is cooked. Drizzle with syrup. It's heavenly! *(For a firmer texture, use bread with more substance like brioche.)* **MUG**

# Nacho Mug Olé

¼ C. refried beans

¼ C. salsa

¼ tsp. coarse black pepper

Multigrain or other hefty tortilla chips

2 T. canned diced green chiles

½ C. diced tomato, plus more for serving

½ C. shredded Mexican cheese blend, plus more for the top

Avocado

Sour cream

## Directions

In a small bowl, mix refried beans, salsa, and black pepper.

In an ungreased mug, make a layer of chips, refried bean mixture, chiles, diced tomato, and cheese; repeat layers. Add another layer of chips, refried beans, chiles, and tomato. Go ahead and fill that mug nearly to the top.

Microwave on high for 60 to 75 seconds or until it's heated through. Then toss on a little more cheese and microwave 30 seconds more so it's nice and melty.

Add some extra diced tomato, a little diced avocado, and a bit of sour cream to top it off. Enjoy immediately. MUG

Hefty tortilla chips will stand up to microwaving a little better than thinner chips.

# Loaded Sweet Potato

1 C. peeled & diced
sweet potato

1 tsp. water

½ C. chopped fresh
broccoli

1 T. chopped onion

1 tsp. minced garlic

1½ tsp. olive oil

¼ tsp. coarse salt

⅛ tsp. coarse black pepper

⅛ tsp. red pepper flakes

3 cherry tomatoes, halved

Shredded Parmesan cheese

1 bacon strip, cooked &
crumbled

## Directions

Grease a mug and put the diced sweet potato and water
inside. Cover with vented plastic wrap and microwave on high
for 4 minutes.

Add the chopped broccoli and onion, minced garlic, and oil.
Cover again with vented plastic wrap and microwave on high
for 60 seconds or until the broccoli is crisp-tender.

Stir in the salt, black pepper, red pepper flakes, and tomato
halves. Sprinkle with cheese and crumbled bacon. MUG

 *It can't be over-stated: beware of
steam when removing plastic wrap!*

# Granola-Stuffed Apple

1 red baking apple

2 heaping T. granola cereal

1½ tsp. brown sugar

¼ tsp. cinnamon

Honey, optional

## Directions

Core the apple without cutting through the bottom and set it in a greased mug.

Cover with vented plastic wrap and microwave on high for 90 seconds.

Stir together the cereal, brown sugar, and cinnamon and stuff it into the cavity of the apple. Cover again with vented plastic wrap and microwave on high 90 seconds more or until the apple is soft. Let stand for 2 minutes.

Drizzle on a little honey, if you'd like. There may be some juice in the bottom of your mug, so make sure you include it when eating your apple. MUG

*There's no faster way to "bake" an apple than in your microwave. You'll still get all of the cinnamon-y apple fragrance and flavor!* TIP

# Balsamic Pasta Salad

½ C. pipette pasta

½ C. warm water

Pinch of salt

⅓ C. chopped yellow
bell pepper

⅓ C. seeded & chopped
tomato

⅓ C. chopped cucumber

1 T. olive oil

½ tsp. balsamic vinegar

¼ tsp. lemon pepper
seasoning

¼ tsp. garlic salt

## Directions

In an ungreased mug, combine uncooked pasta, water, and salt. Set mug in the microwave on a double layer of paper towels. Microwave on high for 2 minutes; stir. Microwave on high 2 minutes more and stir again. If the pasta isn't quite tender, give it another 60 seconds in the microwave.

Stir in the chopped bell pepper, tomato, and cucumber. Stir in the oil and vinegar. Let it set a few minutes to cool slightly, and then stir in the lemon pepper seasoning and garlic salt. MUG

TIP *You can eat this salad either warm or at room temperature.*

# Blueberry Muffin

1½ T. softened butter, divided

2 tsp. quick-cooking oats

1½ tsp. plus 1 T. brown sugar, divided

1 T. plus ¼ C. flour, divided

Pinch of ground allspice

¼ tsp. cinnamon, divided

¼ tsp. baking powder

⅛ tsp. salt

2 T. milk

1 T. frozen blueberries

## Directions

In a small bowl, stir together 1 tablespoon butter, uncooked oats, 1½ teaspoons brown sugar, 1 tablespoon flour, allspice, and ⅛ teaspoon cinnamon; set aside.

In a greased mug, mix baking powder, salt, and remaining brown sugar, flour, and cinnamon. Add remaining butter and mash with a fork. Stir in the milk until well blended; scrape down the side of the mug and push blueberries into the batter. Top with oats mixture. Microwave on high for 90 seconds or until muffin tests done with a toothpick.

## Keep some on hand

For muffins, stir together 1 T. baking powder, 1½ tsp. salt, 3 C. flour, ¾ C. brown sugar, and 1½ tsp. cinnamon. For streusel, stir together ½ C. oats, 6 T. brown sugar, ¾ C. flour, ¾ tsp. allspice, & 1½ tsp. cinnamon. Store in separate airtight containers. To make 1 muffin, stir together ⅓ C. muffin mix, ½ T. softened butter, and 2 T. milk as directed above; add berries. Stir together 2 T. streusel mix and 1 T. softened butter; add to top of batter. Microwave as directed above. MUG

# Cheesy Veggie Soup

1 tsp. butter

¼ C. diced smoked sausage

¼ C. chopped onion

⅛ tsp. caraway seed

Black pepper, cayenne pepper, and garlic salt to taste

1 bay leaf

½ C. chicken broth

¼ C. diced peeled potatoes

¼ C. chopped fresh broccoli florets

¼ C. chopped fresh cauliflower florets

2 tsp. heavy cream

3 T. shredded cheddar cheese

## Directions

Put butter, diced sausage, chopped onion, caraway seed, black pepper, cayenne pepper, garlic salt, and bay leaf in an ungreased mug.

Microwave on high for 2 minutes, stirring halfway through cooking time. Add broth, diced potatoes, and chopped broccoli and cauliflower.

Microwave on high for 5 minutes or until veggies are crisp-tender, stirring every minute or two. Stir in the cream and microwave on high 60 seconds more or until heated through. Discard bay leaf. Add cheese and stir until melted. MUG

*Use the caraway seed in this recipe. It adds a unique hint of flavor to this more traditional soup.*

# Index